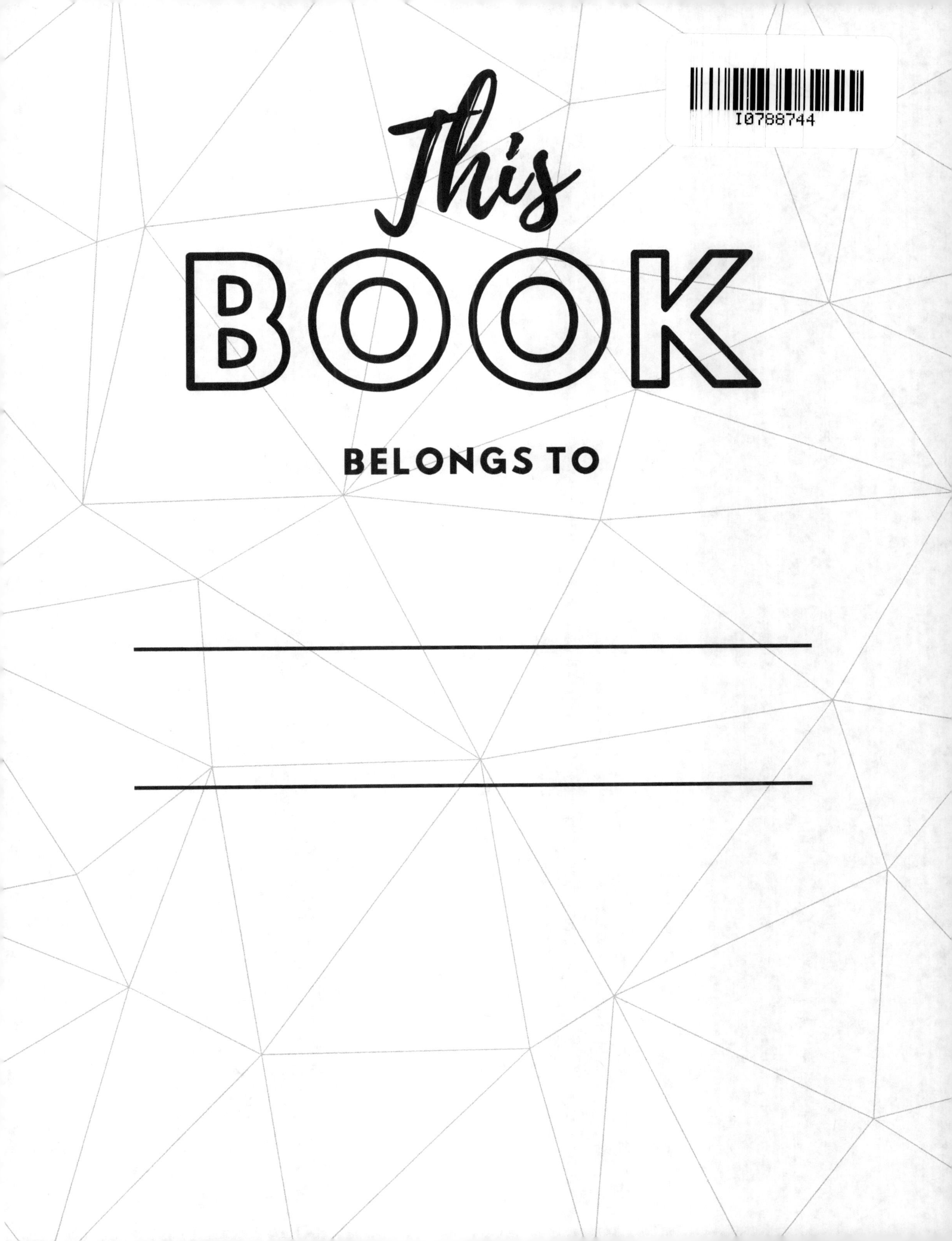

This
BOOK
BELONGS TO

Color TEST

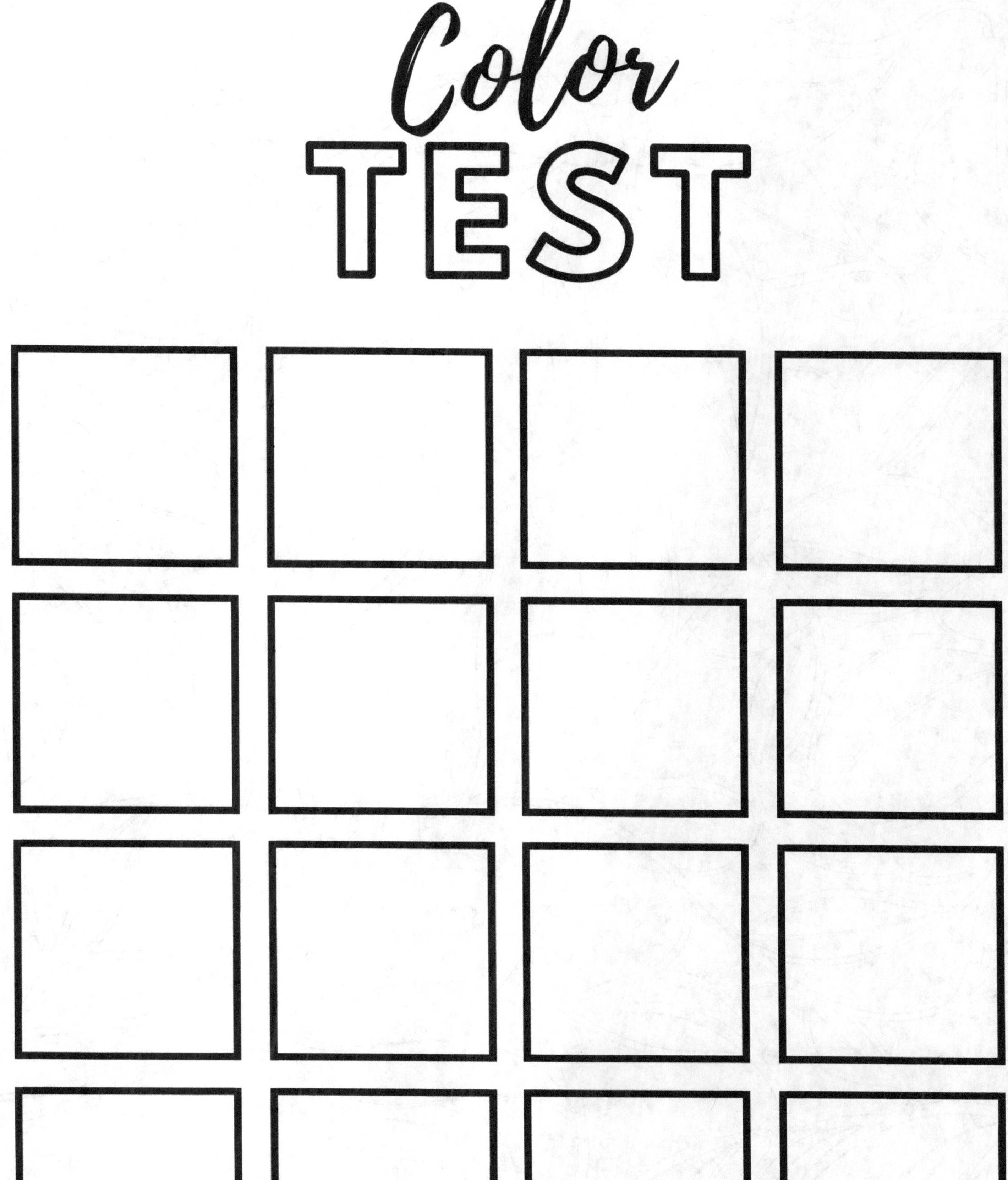

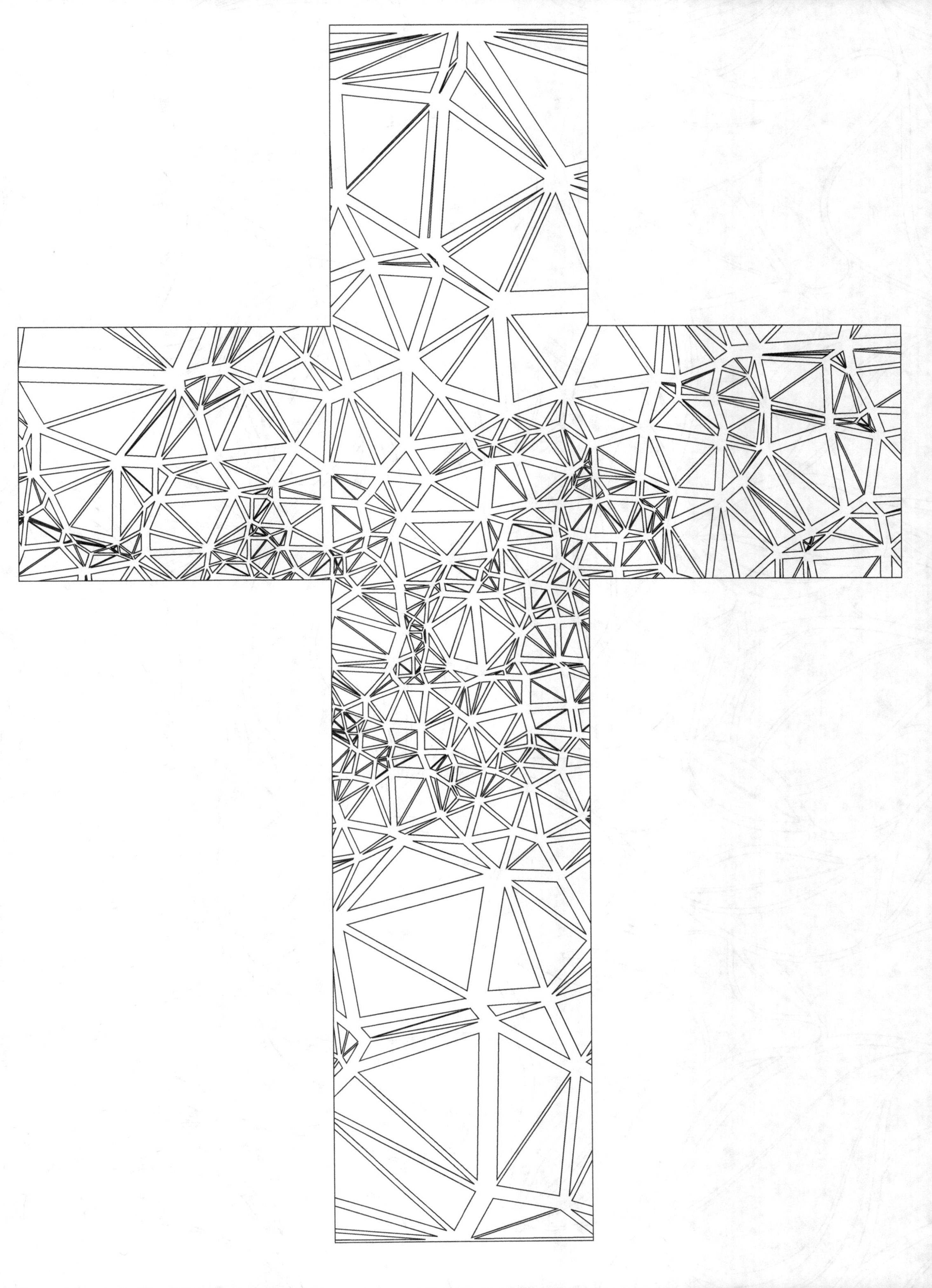

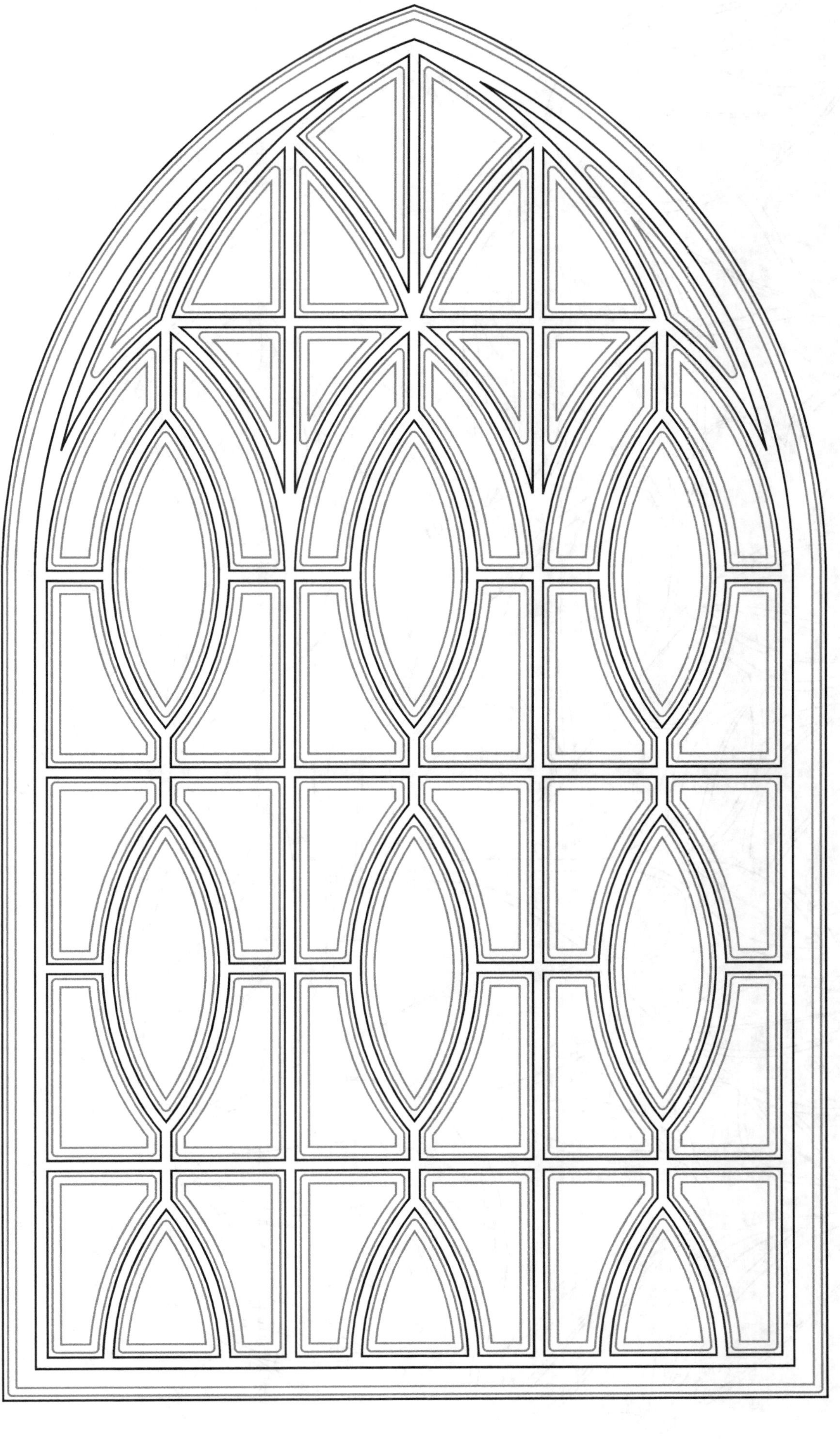

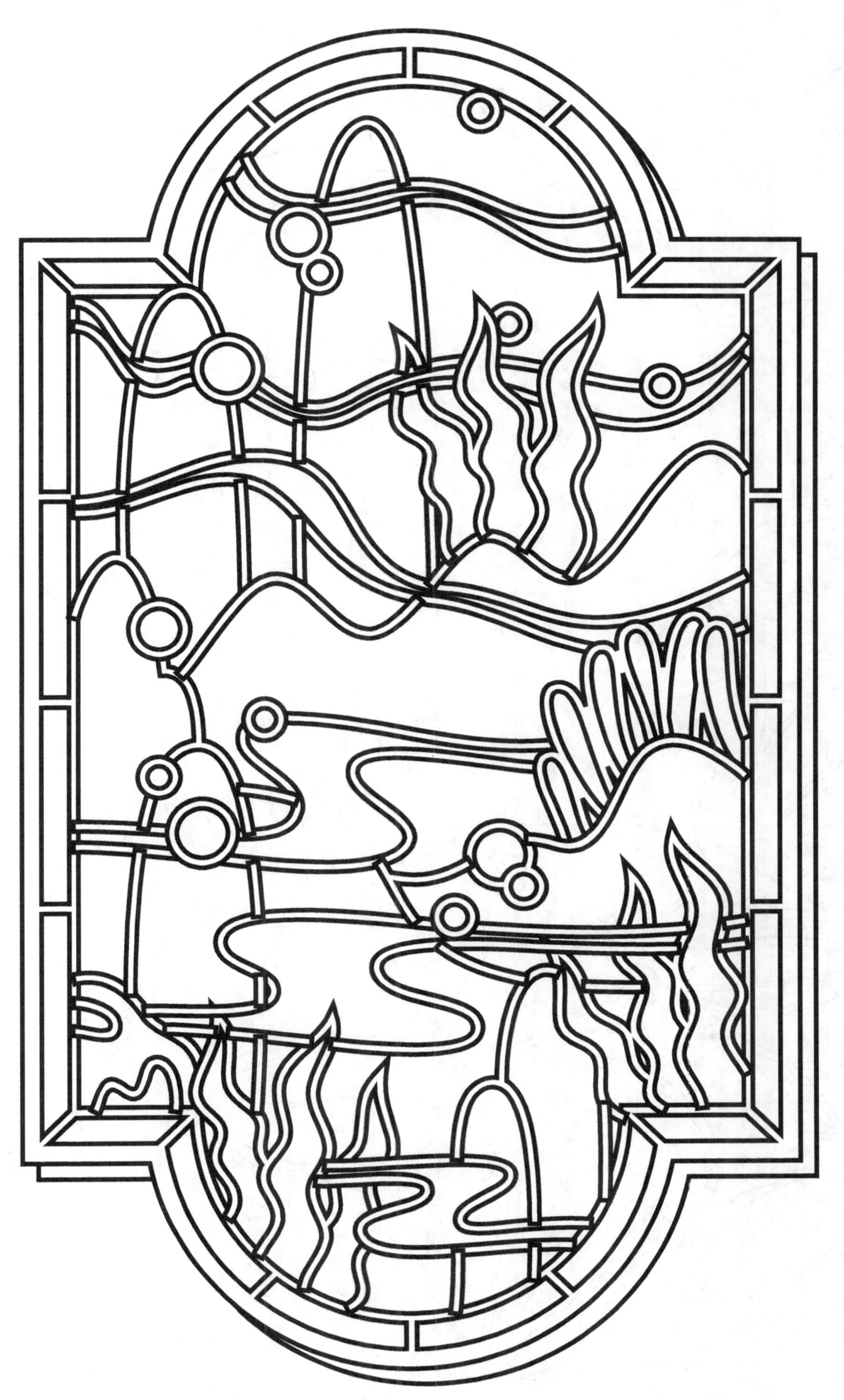

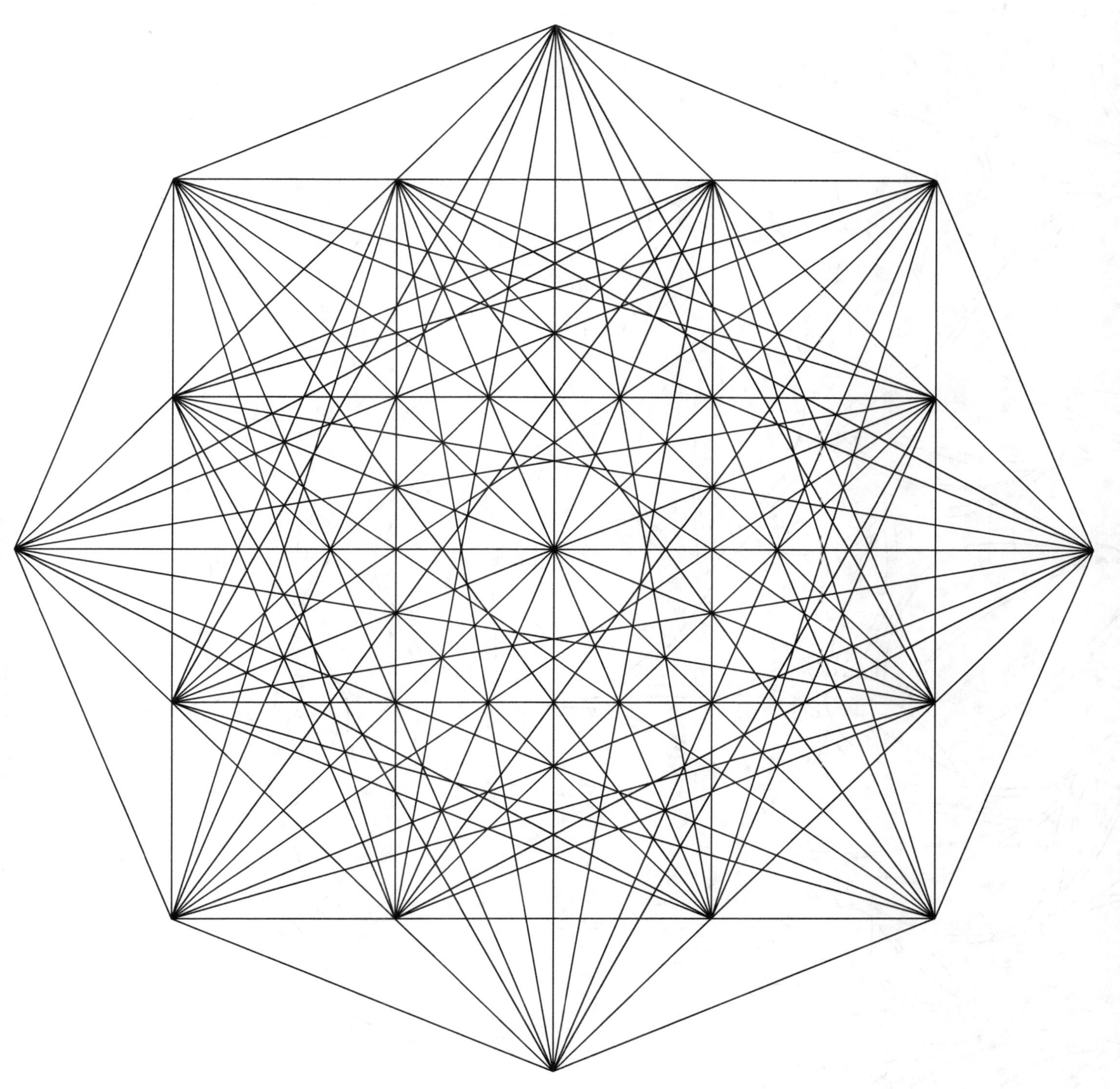